Alpha to Omega 10

Dracula

Bram Stoker

Retold by Diana Birkbeck

A Birkbeck Oxford Series

Heinemann

Heinemann Educational Publishers
Halley Court, Jordan Hill, Oxford OX2 8EJ
A division of Reed Educational and Professional Publishing Ltd

OXFORD MELBOURNE AUCKLAND
JOHANNESBURG BLANTYRE GABORONE
IBADAN PORTSMOUTH (NH) USA CHICAGO

03 02 01 00 99
10 9 8 7 6 5 4 3 2 1

ISBN 0 435 10447 0

Designed and produced by Artistix
Illustrations by Graham Howells
Cover design by Artistix
Printed and bound in the UK by Thomson Litho Ltd

Tel: 01865 888058 email: info.he@heinemann.co.uk

The story you are about to read is a strange and terrible one. It tells of vampires, the undead souls who suck the blood of the living by night, and at daybreak return to their coffins to sleep. Once bitten, their victims turn into vampires themselves. Vampires fear nothing but a crucifix and the smell of garlic.

In May 1850, a young man named Jonathan Harker set out for the wild mountains of Transylvania. He had business there with a certain Count Dracula. The terrible events that followed are recorded in the diaries of Jonathan and his girlfriend.

Jonathan's diary

May 4th, Transylvania

I felt uneasy as we travelled higher into the mountains. It was midnight as we entered the Borgo Pass where a coach was waiting for us. When I saw the driver's face, my heart sank, for he was a fearful-looking man. He wore a great black hat and had teeth which seemed oddly sharp.

I fell asleep as soon as I entered the coach and awoke as we arrived at a huge, grim castle.

The great door was opened by a thin, tall man with a face as pale as death.

'Count Dracula?' I asked.

'I am,' said he, and his hand in mine was as cold as ice. Then he left me, saying that he would be away till the next day.

May 5th

I slept little that night and had bad dreams. It was still dark when I awoke. I had just begun to shave when I felt a hand on my arm. I turned to see the Count behind me – but there was no reflection in the mirror! I got such a shock that I cut myself on my razor so that the blood ran down my face. When the Count saw the blood, he seemed to go mad and grabbed me around the neck. Then he felt my crucifix and quickly let me go.

'You have cut yourself,' he said, and left.

When I got over my shock, I set out to explore the castle. Every door was locked – the only way out of here is by the windows! Then I heard the castle door thud. The Count had come back. I crept to my room and through the crack in the door I saw him make my bed. There are no servants here! We are alone.

May 12th

Late this evening, I saw a fearful thing. As I looked from my window, I saw below me the Count, crawling down the castle walls like a huge lizard. I must escape!

May 28th

I have been trapped in this castle for two weeks now and haven't seen another soul. Nor have I seen the Count in the daytime. Does he sleep by day? When does he eat and drink? I must find out!

June 30th

The only way into the Count's room is by the window, so I climbed out, down a gutter, until I reached it. I found myself in an old chapel. On the floor were some big wooden boxes, filled with earth, which gave off a sickly smell. They were coffins! Then my heart stopped, for in one of the coffins lay the Count. I grabbed a spade to kill him with but he woke up and turned towards me!

The next part of Jonathan Harker's diary is missing. But the story continues in the diary of Mina, Jonathan's girlfriend.

July 24th, Yorkshire

I am staying with Lucy. She will marry her Arthur soon. It makes me a little sad for I have not had news of Jonathan for more than a month.

Lucy is not well. She is very pale and restless, and walks in her sleep. What can be wrong?

August 8th

A ship was wrecked on the rocks here last night. It was very strange. There was nobody on board, only a dead man lashed to the wheel! They say there were a lot of big wooden boxes in the hold.

August 11th

Lucy is in grave danger. Last night I found her in the graveyard! A long, black shape was bent over her. It flew off when it saw me, but there were little red marks on her neck which will not stop bleeding.

August 17th

I called in the doctor to see Lucy, who gets weaker and paler every day. When he saw the marks on her neck, he went very quiet and said we must never leave her alone. He came back the next day with a big bunch of garlic flowers!

August 18th

Alas! Lucy is dead! Last night her mother took away the garlic flowers and opened the window to get rid of the smell, and the black thing must have got in to Lucy! She has left a note saying something about a huge bat.

September 22nd, London

Jonathan is back, thank goodness! He has been ill. Something terrible has happened to him, but he cannot tell me.

September 24th

I have read Jonathan's diary. Can it be true? I fear for us all, for Count Dracula has been seen in London!

September 30th

Alas, everything in Jonathan's diary is true! Yesterday, the doctor came to see us with some terrible news.

There have been reports in the papers about children being attacked in London. All of them had small bite marks on their necks.

'Those marks were made by Lucy,' the doctor told us.

She had turned into a vampire!

'I had to act quickly,' he went on. 'Arthur and I went to the churchyard and opened her grave. In the coffin lay Lucy's body, but the face was that of a vampire. Arthur drove a stake into its black heart and Lucy is at rest at last. But we must destroy Dracula! There is only one way: to purify the coffins so that he has nowhere to rest. Will you help me?'

We made a vow to find Dracula and destroy him for ever.

Here Mina's diary ends. The story is continued in Jonathan's diary.

October 1st, London

Good news and bad. We found the coffins – all but one. The doctor, Arthur and myself put a holy wafer into each coffin and purified the earth inside. We got home after dark to find – oh horror! – Dracula, standing by Mina's bed, holding her by the neck. Her nightdress had drops of blood on it. The vampire fled when it saw my crucifix, but Mina has been bitten and we know what that means. The only way to save her is to destroy Dracula. We think he has left for Transylvania in the coffin we could not find. We must go after him.

October 2nd

Dracula will have to go by sea because of his coffin. If we go by land, we will catch him up. Mina is not well, there is no time to lose.

November 5th

The Count travels fast. He knows we are following him. If he reaches the castle before us, all is lost.

November 11th, Transylvania

Late this afternoon, the doctor, Arthur and myself entered the Borgo Pass on horseback. It was icy cold and snow was falling. Suddenly we saw some men above us, driving a cart with a great box on it.

We whipped our horses and went after it, shouting to the men to stop. They flashed their knives at us but the doctor held them at gunpoint while I pulled the lid off the coffin. In it the vampire lay pale as death in the earth. I drove my knife into its heart, the eyes turned red with hate, then the whole body turned to dust.

Above us, we saw Castle Dracula, black against the red sky of the sunset. We were only just in time! Mina is saved and the Curse of Dracula is destroyed for ever.

Word list

This story is suitable for use when pupils have reached page 182 of the *Alpha to Omega Handbook.*

There are a number of words in the story that are taught beyond page 182 of the *Alpha to Omega Handbook.* Those that students may find difficult to *read* are included in the 'Harder words' list below.

Words and phrases special to the story

1 Jon/a/than Harker
2 Tran/syl/va/nia
3 Count Dra/cu/la
4 Borgo Pass
5 Mina
6 Lucy
7 Arthur

Harder words

1 story
2 vampires
3 blood
4 cru/ci/fix
5 mountains
6 razor
7 wrong
8 doctor
9 quiet
10 pur/i/fy
11 pur/i/fied
12 whipped